The Ulti

<u>Relationships</u>

Communication In Relationships To Handle Dysfunctional Relationships And Create Lasting Relationships For Life!

Mia Conrad

STOP!!! Before you read any further....Would you like to know the Secrets of Transforming your life, overcome insecurities, develop leadership skills, and undeniable confidence in your personal, professional, and relationship life?

If your answer is yes, then you are not alone. Thousands of people are looking for the secret to have unstoppable confidence and self-driven power in all areas of their lives.

If you have been searching for these answers without much luck, you're in the right place!

Not only will you gain incredible insight in this book, but because I want to make sure to give you as much value as possible, right now for a limited time you can get full **100% FREE access to a VIP bonus EBook** entitled **LIMITLESS ENERGY!**

Just Go Here For Free Instant Access:

www.PotentialRise.com

Legal Notice

Disclaimer Notice

information contained herein on the new conditions whenever they see applicable.

Table Of Contents

Introduction

I want to thank you and congratulate you for purchasing the book, *"Relationships: The Ultimate Guide To Better Relationships! - Communication In Relationships To Handle Dysfunctional Relationships And Create Lasting Relationships for Life!"*.

This book contains proven steps and strategies on how to strengthen and create new relationships in your life. Through using this book, it is my hope that your current relationships will be stronger than you ever thought imaginable and your future relationships will start off with the right foot forward!

Your relationships can still improve and be strengthened. Also, there's much room in your life for brand new bonds. Through this book, you'll be able to learn the essentials of having lasting relationships in a simple manner.

Thanks again for purchasing this book, I hope you enjoy it!

Chapter 1 – What Weakens & Destroys Relationships?

Relationships are fragile before they are robust; before they're strong enough to withstand various challenges. Perhaps one of the reasons why you've downloaded this book is due to a weakening relationship. It may be that some of your relationships are already nearly ruined because of the factors enumerated below. These are among the top reasons why many relationships fail. They're wide-encompassing, so it's best to detect them as early as possible.

Pride

Pride is the root of many destructive things. Some say that pride can sometimes be helpful in pulling yourself up and defending yourself during a conflict. However, it's a dangerous thing to play with. Many relationships are ruined when neither of the parties of sides is willing to approach the matter with humility. It's not your fault you couldn't make it to your friend's party, not your fault you couldn't visit your grumpy father. You may have caused someone great pain, yet are unwilling to seek his forgiveness.

Maybe someone hurt you in the past and despite their sincere apology, forgiving them seems impossible. Perhaps there was a time when you needed help, yet you didn't ask because you thought you could handle it. The project failed and you started to blame your friend for not sensing your need for assistance. As you can see, pride more often creates rifts between people than builds one's character up. It's something that you must do away with as soon as possible.

Pride transcends immediate relationships and affects future bonds as well. If you want to create healthy and sturdy relationships in the future, seriously consider becoming more selfless and generous.

Selfishness

It's quite clear that self-centeredness doesn't aid in strengthening any type of relationship. Unfortunately, many are unaware of the long-lasting effects their selfishness has. When you continuously focus on your needs, not on those around you, your world becomes smaller. In your little world, you don't have to worry about anyone else. In your little world, you're the only inhabitant and it's a very lonely existence.

If you want to avoid weakening—and ultimately destroying—your relationships, it's time to become selfless. Selfishness may seem easy to sustain, but it can quickly take a toll on all your relationships. Since an individual most likely can't choose when to be selfish if it's already become a habit, be careful of your thoughts, words, and actions. Self-centeredness can easily weaken even relationships that have a solid foundation. In time, as most of your efforts are directed to your own welfare, your loved ones will grow weary of keeping the relationship afloat.

You're missing out on a lot of things if your lenses are focused on your little world. It's simply not worth it. Once you start looking at the needs of others, though, you'll help address insecurities and low self-esteem.

Low Self-Esteem or Insecurity

Your friend, partner, or relative may be insecure and unconfident because of your own shortcomings. Of course, they're partly responsible for what they're going through. However, as the supposed other half of the relationship, it's your job to know that their continued lack of confidence can adversely impact your relationship now and in the future. When there's a shortage of self-esteem, people tend to become push-overs, weak-willed, and very needy.

It's exhausting to be in a relationship constituted by insecurities. Preserving and developing trust and joy becomes a nearly impossible feat because there's not much to work with. There are simply too many gaps that need to be filled. The odd thing is these aren't even really gaps, but unrealized potential or untapped confidence. Your loved one may not be receiving enough affirmations from you or from his other friends and relatives. He may be going through a tough time in the office because of a demanding superior. No matter the cause of the insecurity, the effects on a relationship are still destructive in nature.

Weak relationships that are doomed to fail are grounded on pride, selfishness, and low self-esteem. These are the things each and every individual must avoid in order to succeed in creating and strengthening their relationships. Now that you know what to avoid, it's time to learn what to look for in order to have better relationships now and in the future.

Chapter 2 – What Constitutes Strong Relationships?

Strengthening relationships may not be as complicated as advanced physics, but it does require much work and patience. Bonds that can stand the test of time don't grow overnight. Rather, they're the fruit of constant and meaningful communication, trust, and joy. Remember that "it takes two to tango," so it definitely is necessary to contribute to the growth of your relationships. After all, you can't expect something to thrive if you're not taking care of it.

Consistent and Meaningful Communication

Communication is one of the strong pillars holding up any type of relationship. With the constant possibility of misunderstanding one another, it's odd that many people aren't communicating more as the years pass by. It's observable, though, that frequent and meaningful communication is common in strong relationships. Partners, friends, spouses, and relatives eventually find common ground during a conflict and resolve the issue as soon as they can. They're willing to voice out their opinions and hear what the other person has to say.

Communication isn't only useful in resolving disputes, though. It's equally effective in developing lasting bonds. You get the opportunity to become more familiar with someone's likes and dislikes; why he's behaving in a certain way and why he thinks in a certain manner. Do remember that communication is an exchange of thoughts. This means listening and speaking are necessary. You can't call something a conversation if you're the only one talking or listening. It has to be a healthy form of familiarization; a process through which understanding for both sides is deepened.

Trust

Trust is like a very thin wine glass. It's very fragile and once it breaks, it's virtually impossible to piece back together again. Well, you can exert much effort to glue it back together, but it's no longer the same glass. In the same way, once trust is lost in a relationship, the bond is doomed to crumble or dissolve. Weak and unhealthy relationships lack trust and neither side is making a way for the trust to be regained. However, it's quite the opposite in resilient and thriving relationships.

Partners, husbands and wives, friends, co-workers, classmates, and relatives depend on a solid layer of trust for their relationships to grow. If you don't trust your loved one, can you honestly say there's even love at all? Well, maybe. However, this love may slowly be dissipating due to the lack of confidence in the relationship. For example, if a man is caught cheating on his wife, the wife may still love the man. Sadly, she no longer trusts him. Quite possible, she may never trust him again. The bond is strained and any hopes for a better future is ruined.

The people you'll be meeting in the future will also make you work to earn their trust. Once you break that trust, you'll most likely lose it forever. If you want to create great relationships and preserve the ones you have, treasure and take care of the trust others have given to you.

Joy

Everyone will definitely say that every successful and strong relationship is a joy-filled one. Joy magnifies the positives and eradicates the adverse elements in any type of bond. If you have joy in your relationship, it will certainly thrive and last. Unfortunately, due to numerous shortcomings, many relationships nowadays lack genuine joy. They think they're happy just because they're laughing and smiling. Unfortunately, this laughter may just be a facade of what's actually happening.

Joy is different from happiness. Just because someone's laughing their heart out, it does not mean they're joyful. It just means that, at that moment in time, they're happy. Maybe someone made a joke and they found it funny. After the merry-making, they're sad once again. The absence of a clown means the absence of laughter. While happiness is situational, joy is constant. It's developed through a consistent effort to make the relationship work by providing the needs and satisfying the desires of the people in the bond.

To have joy in a relationship, both sides must work together to reach such a goal. It's not going to be easy, but the best things in life are worth the sacrifice and hard work. The next chapters will show you how to apply these principles in each of the main areas in your life. Whether it's your family, boyfriend or girlfriend, or friend, there's always a way to make the pastures greener and the moments sweeter than before.

Chapter 3 – Creating Lasting Friendships

Finding the right friends are among the greatest desires of both men and women. No one wants to be alone and other than your immediate family, it's natural for you to seek bonds elsewhere. So how will you create lasting friendships? Also, how can you strengthen the friendships you already have been blessed with? Some find it difficult to associate with others. In the fast-paced age of the Internet, traditional avenues towards meeting new people have somehow been put aside. This isn't advisable because talking to someone face to face still beats online chat rooms. Take note of the following to learn how to make new friends.

Be Genuine

Fake items have always been less desirable compared to original labels. You would certainly choose a genuine Louis Vuitton over a fake one. In the same way, people don't like "fakers." In a way, the general population seriously dislikes individuals lacking genuineness. If you're aiming to have real friends, then be real. Don't hide behind a fake identity or personality. Sooner or later, people will find out and your true self will be revealed. If you don't even have confidence in who you are, how can people be drawn to you? If you don't love who you are, how can it be easier for others to love you?

Genuineness is your gift to yourself and to all the people you'll be meeting along the way. Show them who you really are so that you can also see who will stay round and accept you for who you are. Unconditional love considerably strengthens a relationship and it paves the way to even better bonds. If the people you're with don't even know that you hate the music they're listening to—you're just pretending to like it—is that real friendship? You're not even being honest to them and you appear to lack enough respect to let them know what you think of their taste in music.

Be Open-Minded

No one's telling you to criticize anyone's preferences, though. You should still respect what others like and just be open-minded. Individuals with closed minds give their loved ones a hard time. They strongly cling to what they believe is true despite the presence of evidences that disprove it. They may always think they're right, never yielding to anyone in each and every argument. Close-minded individuals are no fun to be with. You may see that these people are often isolated due to their refusal to participate in various activities.

Conforming to the norms of the society can sometimes be unhealthy and inadvisable. However, there are times when you should actually consider what others are saying. Open yourself up to other possibilities so that life will be more colorful and your relationships more interesting. Try something new with someone. Go on a road-trip, eat exotic dishes, and participate in interesting and safe activities. Allow excitement into your life and you'll gain many new friends.

Be Supportive and Encouraging

Both old and new friends require a certain degree of encouragement and support. This world is filled with so many discouraging things and it can be argued that saddening things far outnumber the uplifting ones. Your friends have enough situations and people in their lives to beat them down and remind them of their shortcomings. This is why it's your job as their friend to have their backs and remind them of their strengths and talents. If you want to gain new great friends, be a great friend. Be a channel of encouragement, not mockery.

Some people don't even make an effort to push their friends forward. Since they're already quite close, teasing and discouragements somehow become more common than affirmations. You may say that these people are just joking, but jokes hold a hint of truth and the recipient of these may be taking the statements to heart. Your words can either build someone up or tear them down. In some cases, the discouraging words uttered often have long-lasting effects that can be seen even several years after they were said. Don't take your friends for granted and don't think that discouraging anyone—even through a joke—is acceptable.

Chapter 4 – Well-Built Romance

From friendship, two people can head to romance. It may be ideal for most to have a less rocky trip together in a romantic relationship. Unfortunately, it just gets more complicated the deeper two people go. It's safe to assume that romantic relationships are among the most difficult types of relationship to maintain, strengthen, and protect. There are simply too many factors at play and most couples fail to realize what they should do before it's too late. The principles provided below may not answer all the questions you have, but they address the main concerns couples generally face at present.

Avoid the "Fast-Forward" Button

Many couples nowadays are focused on hastening things that they miss out on all the great things they could have experienced together. Romance is a very complex world, which is more often driven by emotions instead of wisdom and rationality. If you want to have a better relationship with your partner, it's necessary to take things slowly. Everything must be done moderately so that you can clearly see how things are progressing.

Most relationships fail because people are tempted by the "fast-forward button." They want things to develop fast so that they can have someone beside them; someone to cuddle with and open yourself up to. Unfortunately, in some cases, one or both sides realize that they don't complement each other. They see that they're not right for each other, so they part ways as strangers. This is very disappointing and honestly, a waste of time and energy. If you want to have a great and healthy relationship with someone, you must make time to get to know who that person really is.

Be Attentive and Listen

Other than taking the time to get to know your partner, it's also important to have open ear, eyes, heart, and mind. Attentiveness is a hard quality to develop and use nowadays because people generally lack the patience to listen to someone for a long time. You're lucky if you can have a stranger listen to your story for a few minutes. Sadly, even couples have difficulty in having a real conversation. Either one of the two is too busy or both are just preoccupied with other tasks or thoughts. Being a good listener is what can save, strengthen, and develop your romantic relationship, though.

Once you listen to someone, you're giving them the gift of time, your time. You can't turn back time and you can't get back the time lost. Your partner may be aware of this and he or she's pleased and happy for what you're doing. Your sacrifices will be rewarded and you'll eventually see the fruits of your labor. Strong relationships may not grow on trees, but they require hard work, patience, and an ever-attentive ear and heart. Listen to what your other half is saying and you'll be afforded the same courtesy. It's not easy, especially at the beginning. However, it is crucial to the present and future development of your relationship. Even if you're not in a relationship right now, you can use this principle for your future one.

Seek to Serve, Not to Be Served

This may go against the general notion today that you must look after yourself, your welfare or how your partner is treating you. Well, relationships that last a lifetime are not comprised of two individuals solely seeking their own happiness and satisfaction. Rather, these bonds are formed by two people willing to put the other person first. This must serve as a reminder for husbands and wives and even for those in a long-term relationship. If you put your loved one's needs and interest before yours, you'll be in a better position with him or her.

This isn't about pitying yourself or putting yourself behind each and every time, though. It's about being selfless enough to think about how a certain decision, action, or word will affect your partner. Will your decision to work in a different state or country help you both to have a better relationship? Will your credit card purchases help your spouse deal with the monthly bills? You can serve your loved one in so many ways. You can put gas in the car after you use it, prepare the kids' meals sometimes, buy flowers, or do the dishes. For the unmarried couples, you can have a better relationship if you allow each other to see a different and new area of your life. You can serve your boyfriend or girlfriend by allowing them to see a different side of your life.

Chapter 5 – Harmony In The Family

The family most probably has the most drama and complications in all the relationships one has. Your family is your greatest joy and it can also be your greatest burden. Those closest to you are the ones you need to take care of the most, after all. It shouldn't be a pain, though, to strengthen or improve your relationship with your parents, spouse, children, aunts, uncles, cousins, and even grandparents. There's always a reason to create new bonds within your family. Yes, you can create new connections in your family. If the old way of looking at or regarding each other no longer works, it's time to put on a new set of lenses and have a fresh start.

Resolve Disputes Immediately

There are more conflicts in the family than anyone is willing to admit and count. It's normal to have arguments every now and then. Actually, it's these conflicts that make the wonderful moments even more wonderful. When you're having fun with your relatives, you can remember when you were all going through a tough time. There may have been a time when you were not paying heed to each other because you had a disagreement. Problems exist and they will continue to challenge the strength of your family's bond.

Despite this fact, it's necessary to resolve your disputes immediately. Don't go to sleep till you haven't resolved things with your relative. If it's not possible to solve the conflict today, try tomorrow. Just don't put it off so long because the longer it takes for you to solve the issue, the harder it gets. Forgiveness and reconciliation don't get nearer as time progresses. They just become more unreachable. If you want to have a stronger relationship with your family, let go of the bitterness and actively explore ways to address the concerns before you.

Understand that Differences Exist

Maybe you and your dad have not talked for a very long time—maybe even years. This can be due to the presence of differences between the two of you. You're simply too different and your personalities clash more often than you can tolerate. Well, you can't change who your father is, but you can change the way you approach and perceive the situation. Once you realize that you and your dad will always have differences, you'll behave differently.

This comprehension of the dynamics of human interaction can only come from a more mature perspective in life. Yes, you require maturity to have a better relationship with your family and with every other person in your life. Even your future family—future spouse and children—will be affected by your understanding of the existence of differences among loved ones. Your similarities may be helpful in keeping you together, but it's your contrasting qualities that make your life more colorful.

Support Your Loved One's Dreams
Your present and future family—if you're not married yet—also require your constant support. Your siblings, parents, spouse, kids, and other relatives would certainly want you to support them in reaching their goals. It's not easy to attain big aspirations, especially when there are numerous challenges before you. For certain, you'd also want their support whenever you're trying to get to the finish line of your own goal. Your support will always be appreciated even if your relatives may not be clearly showing it.

Love is clearly seen through continued support and encouragement. If their friends are supporting them, of course they'd want to get your support as well. The relationships in your life can either go down the drain or grow stronger. They depend heavily on your efforts to care for the people in your life. So, will you make an effort to strengthen your current relationships and create new wonderful one?

Conclusion

Thank you again for purchasing this book on how to strengthen your relationships in your life and create incredible new ones!

I am extremely excited to pass this information along to you, and I am so happy that you now have read and can hopefully implement these strategies going forward.

I hope this book was able to help you understand how to strengthen and create amazing relationships in your life!

The next step is to get started using this information and start building those lasting relationships for life.

If you know of anyone else that could benefit from the information presented here please inform them of this book.

Finally, if you enjoyed this book and feel it has added value to your life in any way, please take the time to share your thoughts and post a review on Amazon. It'd be greatly appreciated!

Thank you and good luck!

Preview Of:

<u>Conversation Skills Now!</u>

Ignite Your Life With Proven Conversation Strategies, Communication Skills, And Conversation Power To Create Your Destiny!

Introduction

I want to thank you and congratulate you for purchasing the book, *"Conversation Skills Now! - Ignite Your Life With Proven Conversation Strategies, Communication Skills, And Conversation Power To Create Your Destiny"*.

This book contains insight on the Art of Conversation and how you can use this art to create a life of your choosing.

Picture this; you are standing in an elevator with a middle aged man wearing a Hawaiian shirt, shorts, and boat shoes. You say nothing to him, you do however, think to yourself, "Wow, pretty relaxed attire for a Tuesday afternoon, he must be out of work."

Now consider this, chances are this middle aged man in relaxed attire is not out of work, on the contrary. You see, he is actually the owner of one of the area's finest business enterprises. He is actually so successful that he doesn't have to dress up, but you wouldn't know this, because you didn't bother to talk to him. If you would have spoken to him, you would have found out that he actually was in need of someone like you.

Whether you are young, old, successful, unsuccessful, an entrepreneur, or an employee, you owe it to yourself and your future to learn and apply the art of conversation to your advantage. This book shows you how.

Thanks again for purchasing this book. I hope you enjoy it!

Chapter 1: The Importance Of Conversation

It is said that humans are extremely conversational animals. Other than the ability to think, one of the things that make humans stand out from other animals is their ability to make conversations with others. This ability has proven to be the backbone of society, as interactions between different individuals is very important in forming all kinds of social bonds.

Of course, it is not that conversation is merely a domain reserved for humans. In fact, even other animals have shown their own unique ability to converse. While they don't do it the same way humans do, animals have their own unique way of communicating with each other. These communication skills allow them to form groups for defense, attack, and other kinds of tasks and tactics. Communication has allowed these organisms to have an extra edge in the wild, where numbers and coordination can spell the difference between life and death.

When you look back at human history, it is apparent that humans have utilized the power of communication to the hilt as well. While the earliest humans have languages that are far from the language systems used today, the presence of these communication systems, both written and oral, cannot be denied.

Perhaps more importantly, not only did conversation allowed for talking, but it also allowed for the sharing of history, virtually assuring that the existence of our forefathers will never be forgotten. Oral histories abound in all ethnic groups worldwide, and a lot of them are more or less proven by the presence of relics in different cradles of civilizations. Re-tracing history, and perhaps the interest in tracing it, probably would have not existed without the presence of our innate communication skills.

But while there are many sub-uses of communication, its main value still lies on its ability to bring people closer together thru communication. As you would know by now, the best way to get to know a person is to talk to them. Of course, you can always choose to not talk to them, but you may actually miss out on a life-changing experience.

If there is an everyday skill that you must continually practice, it is your communication skills. Applying the art of conversation to your everyday life can help you create your destiny in ways you never thought possible. In the next chapters, you will learn the different skills you'll need to talk to anyone. You'll also learn how you can cultivate different personality traits that make you an effective conversationalist. And last but not least, this article will teach you how to use your conversational skill as a means to highlight yourself.

Thanks for Previewing My Exciting Book Entitled:

"Conversation Skills Now! Ignite Your Life With Proven Conversation Strategies, Communication Skills, And Conversation Power To Create Your Destiny!"

To purchase this book, simply go to the Amazon Kindle store and simply search:

"CONVERSATION SKILLS NOW"

Then just scroll down until you see my book. You will know it is mine because you will see my name "Mia Conrad" underneath the title.

Alternatively, you can visit my author page on Amazon to see this book and other work I have done. Thanks so much, and please don't forget your free bonuses

DON'T LEAVE YET! - CHECK OUT YOUR FREE BONUSES BELOW!

Free Bonus Offer: Get Free Access To The <u>PotentialRise.com</u> VIP Newsletter!

Once you enter your email address you will immediately get free access to this awesome newsletter!

But wait, right now if you join now for free you will also get free access to the "LIMITLESS ENERGY" free EBook!

To claim both your FREE VIP NEWSLETTER MEMBERSHIP and your FREE BONUS Ebook on LIMITLESS ENERGY!

<u>Just Go To:</u>

www.PotentialRise.com

Made in the USA
Coppell, TX
22 March 2020